December 2004

Merry Ch[...]

Love John & Susan

It Is Well With My Soul

THOMAS KINKADE

HARVEST HOUSE PUBLISHERS
EUGENE, OREGON 97402

It Is Well With My Soul

Copyright © 2001 by Media Arts Group, Inc.,
San Jose, CA 95131
and by Harvest House Publishers,
Eugene, Oregon 97402

ISBN 0-7369-0631-2

Media Arts Group, Inc.
521 Charcot Avenue
San Jose, CA 95131
1.800.366.3733

Scripture quotations are from the Holy Bible, New International Version.
Copyright © 1973, 1978, 1984 by the International Bible Society.
Used by permission of Zondervan Publishing House.

Design and production by Koechel Peterson & Associates, Minneapolis, Minnesota

Printed in Hong Kong

04 05 06 07 08 09 10 / **NG** / 10 9 8 7 6 5 4 3

Y ou will keep in perfect peace him whose mind is steadfast, because he trusts in you. Trust in the Lord forever, for the Lord, the Lord, is the Rock eternal.

—THE BOOK OF ISAIAH—

ever will I leave you; never will I forsake you...
—THE BOOK OF HEBREWS—

Sweet is the promise, "I will not forget thee,"
Nothing can molest or turn my soul away;
E'en tho' the night be dark within the valley,
Just beyond is shining one eternal day.
"I will not forget thee or leave thee;
In My hands I'll hold thee, in My arms I'll fold thee;
I will not forget thee or leave thee;
I am thy Redeemer, I will care for thee."

— CHARLES H. GABRIEL —

O God, our help in ages past,
Our hope for years to come,
Our shelter from the stormy blast,
And our eternal home!

Before the hills in order stood,
Or earth received her frame,
From everlasting Thou art God,
To endless years the same.

BESIDE STILL WATER

O God, our help in ages past,
Our hope for years to come,
Be Thou our guard while life shall last,
And our eternal home.

— ISAAC WATTS —

*F*aith sees the invisible, believes the
unbelievable, and receives the impossible.

— CORRIE TEN BOOM —

*T*hen you will call upon Me and come and
pray to Me, and I will listen to you. You will
seek Me and find Me when you seek Me with
all your heart.

— THE BOOK OF JEREMIAH —

seek

What, then, shall we say in response to this?
If God is for us, who can be against us?

— THE BOOK OF ROMANS —

I need Thee every hour, most gracious Lord;
No tender voice like Thine, can peace afford.
I need Thee, O I need Thee;
Every hour I need Thee!
O bless me now, my Saviour,
I come to Thee.

—ANNIE S. HAWKS—

light of life

I am the light of the world. Whoever
follows Me will never walk in darkness,
but will have the light of life.

—THE BOOK OF JOHN—

When peace, like a river, attendeth my way,

When sorrows like sea billows roll;

Whatever my lot, Thou hast taught me to say,

It is well, it is well with my soul.

—Horatio G. Spafford—

Another day is dawning, dear Master, let it be,
In working or in waiting, another day with Thee.
—Frances R. Havergal—

heart

T rust in the Lord with all your heart
and lean not on your own understanding;
in all your ways acknowledge Him, and He
will make your paths straight.

—THE BOOK OF PROVERBS—

CLEARING STORMS

S aviour, like a shepherd lead us,
Much we need Thy tender care;
In Thy pleasant pastures feed us,
For our use Thy fold prepare.

—DOROTHY A. THRUPP—

souls

C ome to me, all you who are weary and burdened, and I will give you rest. Take my yoke upon you and learn from me, for I am gentle and humble in heart, and you will find rest for your souls. For my yoke is easy and my burden is light.

—THE BOOK OF MATTHEW—

G od writes with a pen that never blots, speaks with a tongue that never slips, and acts with a hand that never fails.

—AUTHOR UNKNOWN—

Abide with me: fast falls the eventide;
The darkness deepens; Lord, with me abide:
When other helpers fail, and comforts flee,
Help of the helpless, O abide with me!

—HENRY F. LYTE—

We must build our faith not on fading lights
but on the Light that never fails.

—OSWALD CHAMBERS—

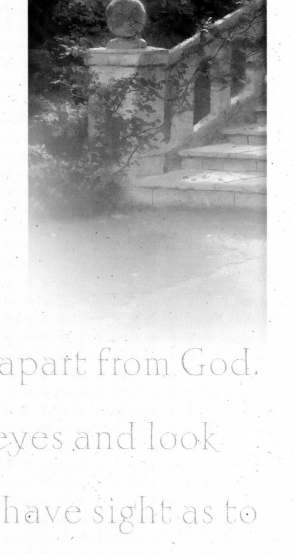

Faith, like sight, is nothing apart from God. You might as well shut your eyes and look inside, and see whether you have sight as to look inside to discover whether you have faith.

—HANNAH WHITALL SMITH—

Faith is like radar that sees through the fog—the reality of things at a distance that the human eye cannot see.

—CORRIE TEN BOOM—

It matters not what tongue we speak,
Nor where life's pathway leads;
God hears the cries His children raise
And always meets our needs.

—DENNIS J. DEHAAN—

Cast your cares on the Lord, and he will sustain you; he will never let the righteous fall.

—THE BOOK OF PSALMS—

Do not be anxious about anything, but in everything, by prayer and petition, with thanksgiving, present your requests to God. And the peace of God, which transcends all understanding, will guard your hearts and your minds…

—THE BOOK OF PHILIPPIANS—

FAITH

BRIDGE OF FAITH

Faith—is the Pierless Bridge
Supporting what We see
Unto the Scene that We do not—.

—EMILY DICKINSON—

For answered prayer, we thank You, Lord,
We know You're always there
To hear us when we call on You;
We're grateful for Your care.

—J. DAVID BRANON—

Prayer is the rustling of the wings of the
angels who are bringing the blessing to us.

—CHARLES SPURGEON—

angels

How blessed and amazing are God's gifts,
dear friends!

—CLEMENT OF ROME—

Nearer, still nearer, close to Thy heart,

Draw me, my Saviour, so precious Thou art;

Fold me, O fold me close to Thy breast,

Shelter me safe in that haven of rest,

Shelter me safe in that haven of rest.

—Mrs. C. H. Morris—

SHELTER

Once we truly see God at work, we will never

be concerned again about the things that happen,

because we are actually trusting in our Father

in heaven, whom the world cannot see.

—Oswald Chambers—

prayer

Prayer is co-operation with God. It is the purest exercise of the faculties God has given us—an exercise that links these faculties with the Maker to work out the intentions He had in mind in their creation. Prayer is aligning ourselves with the purposes of God...

—E. STANLEY JONES—

HOMETOWN EVENING

Pray continually; give thanks in all circumstances, for this is God's will for you...

—THE BOOK OF I THESSALONIANS—

Faith is to believe what you do not see; the reward of this faith is to see what you believe.

—SAINT AUGUSTINE—

believe

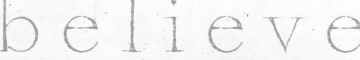

A LIGHT IN THE STORM

The smallest seed of faith is better than the largest fruit of happiness.

—HENRY DAVID THOREAU—

seed

If I rise on the wings of the dawn, if I settle on the far side of the sea, even there Your hand will guide me, Your right hand will hold me fast.

—THE BOOK OF PSALMS—

HEAL

Never a weakness that He does not feel,
Never a sickness that He cannot heal,
Never a sorrow that He does not share,
Moment by moment I'm under His care.

—DANIEL WHITTLE—

THE LIGHT OF PEACE

Seeing our Father in everything makes life
one long thanksgiving and gives rest of the heart.

—HANNAH WHITALL SMITH—

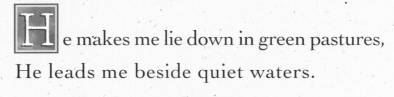

He makes me lie down in green pastures,
He leads me beside quiet waters.

—THE BOOK OF PSALMS—

I will lie down and sleep in peace, for You alone,
O Lord, make me dwell in safety.

—THE BOOK OF PSALMS—

peace

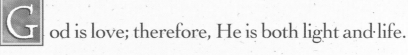

MOONLIT VILLAGE

God is love; therefore, He is both light and life.
A Savior-God! What marvelous grace and glory.

—WILLIAM HALLMAN—

I am convinced that neither death nor life, neither angels nor demons, neither the present nor the future, nor any powers, neither height nor depth, nor anything else in all creation, will be able to separate us from the love of God...

—THE BOOK OF ROMANS—

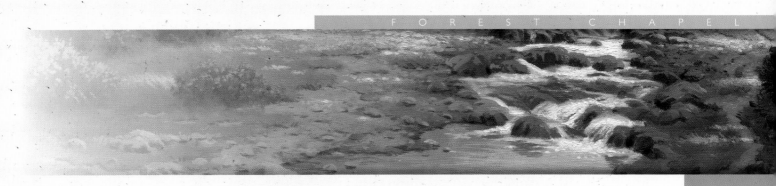

FOREST CHAPEL

LOVE

Immortal Love, forever full,
Forever flowing free,
Forever shared, forever whole,
A never-ebbing sea!

—JOHN G. WHITTIER—

bless

Sweet hour of prayer, sweet hour of prayer,
That calls me from a world of care,
And bids me at my Father's throne,
Make all my wants and wishes known!
In seasons of distress and grief,
My soul has often found relief,
And oft escaped the tempter's snare,
By thy return, sweet hour of prayer.

Sweet hour of prayer, sweet hour of prayer,
Thy wings shall my petition bear
To Him, who truth and faithfulness
Engage the waiting soul to bless:
And since He bids me seek His face,
Believe His word, and trust His grace,
I'll cast on Him my every care,
And wait for thee, sweet hour of prayer.

—W. W. WALFORD—

T hen I saw a new heaven and a new earth… "Now the dwelling of God is with men, and he will live with them. They will be his people, and God himself will be with them and be their God. He will wipe every tear from their eyes. There will be no more death or mourning, or crying or pain, for the old order of things has passed away."

—THE BOOK OF REVELATION—

You know with all your heart and soul that not one of all the good promises the Lord your God gave you has failed. Every promise has been fulfilled; not one has failed.

—THE BOOK OF JOSHUA—

In Christ is found a God who is near,
who hears, who cares, who loves…

—EUGENE REUWELER—

BLOSSOM HILL CHURCH

There is a safe and sacred place
Beneath the wings divine,
Reserved for all the heirs of grace—
Oh, be that refuge mine!

—HENRY F. LYTE—

sacred

The Lord is my light and my salvation—
whom shall I fear?

—THE BOOK OF PSALMS—

TRUST

He who dwells in the shelter of the Most High will rest in the shadow of the Almighty. I will say of the Lord, "He is my refuge and my fortress, my God, in whom I trust."

—THE BOOK OF PSALMS—

PETALS OF HOPE

He hideth my soul in the cleft of the rock
That shadows a dry, thirsty land;
He hideth my life in the depths of His love,
And covers me there with His hand,
And covers me there with His hand.

—FANNY J. CROSBY—

light

And I said to the one who stood at the gate of the year, "Give me a light that I may tread safely into the Unknown." And he replied, "Go out into the darkness and put your hand into the hand of God. That shall be to you better than light and safer than a known way."

—MINNIE HASKINS—

THE SEA OF TRANQUILITY

Even the darkness will not be dark to you;
the night will shine like the day,
for darkness is as light to you.

—THE BOOK OF PSALMS—

Thomas Kinkade

When the trials of this life make you weary
And your troubles seem too much to bear,
There's a wonderful solace and comfort
In the silent communion of prayer.

—AUTHOR UNKNOWN—

GLORIOUS

MOUNTAIN CHAPEL

You are my lamp, O Lord;
the Lord turns my darkness into light.

—THE BOOK OF 2 SAMUEL—

Oh! It is a glorious fact, that prayers are
noticed in heaven.

—CHARLES SPURGEON—

He will show compassion, so
great is his unfailing love...

—THE BOOK OF LAMENTATIONS—

SUNDAY EVENING SLEIGH RIDE

BEAUTY

Lord of the far horizons,
Give us the eyes to see
Over the verge of the sundown
The beauty that is to be.

—BLISS CARMAN—

Our faith comes in moments . . . yet
there is a depth in those brief moments
which constrains us to ascribe more reality
to them than to all other experiences.

—RALPH WALDO EMERSON—

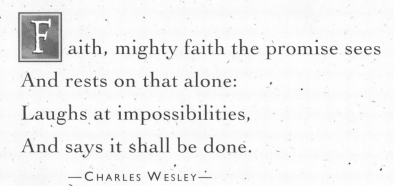

Faith, mighty faith the promise sees
And rests on that alone:
Laughs at impossibilities,
And says it shall be done.

—CHARLES WESLEY—

FAITH

Thomas Kinkade

paintings

He shielded him and cared for him; he guarded him as the apple of his eye, like an eagle that stirs up its nest and hovers over its young, that spreads its wings to catch them and carries them on its pinions...

—THE BOOK OF DEUTERONOMY—